The "Spicer" of Life

D. S. Mullis

AuthorHouse™
1663 Liberty Drive, Suite 200
Bloomington, IN 47403
www.authorhouse.com
Phone: 1-800-839-8640

©2008 D. S. Mullis. All rights reserved.

No part of this book may be reproduced, stored in a retrieval system, or transmitted by any means without the written permission of the author.

First published by AuthorHouse 6/11/2008

ISBN: 978-1-4343-5817-2 (sc)

Printed in the United States of America
Bloomington, Indiana

This book is printed on acid-free paper.

Contents

Section – I Encouragement

A Jewel	3
A Journey	4
Biding One's Time	5
Character	6
Choices	7
Come Walk with Me	8
Focus	9
Folks!	10
God's Majesty	11
Guard Your Heart	12
His Plan	13
It Matters Not	14
It's a Setup!	15
Just 'Round the Bend	16
Letting Go	17
Mercy	18
Moorings	19
Once Again	20
Seasons of Life	21
The Lighthouse	22
The Spicer of Life	23
Until…	24
Words!	25

Section – II Family

A Man after God's Heart	29
A Walk down Memory Lane	30
Be Thankful!	31
Family Life	32
Freedom	33
Kinfolk	34
My Heritage	35
My Mama	36

My Uncle-The Barber	37
My Uncle-The Preacher	38
The Love of a Son	39
The Shop	40
Three Wishes	41

Section – III Friends

As I Go!	45
As You Marry	46
'Becca Jane	47
Covenant Brothers	48
Growing Old	49
Happy 30th Anniversary!	50
Happy 50th Anniversary, Almaleen & Billy!	51
Happy 50th Anniversary, Ellen & Don!	52
Happy 50th Birthday, Brenda!	53
Happy 60th Birthday, Pastor!	54
Happy 90th Birthday!	55
Medicine Lady	56
My Friend	57
Noah!	58
Persevere!	59
Tell Him Who You Are	60
Thank You-Our Seniors!	61
The Blind Lady	62
The Godchaser	63
The Sisters Three	64
What Is a Nurse?	65

Section – IV Grief

A Tribute to "Bubba"	69
In Memory of 'Curly'	70
Our Blessed Hope	71
The Door	72
The Love of God	73
What 'Will' It Be?	74
Where Do We Go From Here?	75

Section – V Hope

Alone with God	79
A Test	80
God Is Love	81
How About Your Heart?	82
How Far?	83
If Only	84
In His Time	85
Life Goes On…	86
Living on the Edge	87
Oh, What a Difference…	88
On We Go…	89
Sacrifice?	90
The Stirring	91
The Toolbox	92
The Way	93
There Is a Rest	94
There's Nothing to Lose	95
What Might Have Been	96
What's that in Your Hand?	97

Section – VI Inspiration & Love

Life Is a Portrait	101
Little Things	102
Only God Knows	103
Passion	104
Shall We Dance?	105
Solitude	106
The Adventure	107
The Back Burner Friend	108
You	109
You Can Make It!	110

Section – VII Prayers

A Daily Prayer	113
A Prayer for You	114
A Secret Hiding Place	115
How Long?	116

Section – VIII Special Days

A Tribute to Mother!	119
Christmas Time	120
Forever Yours!	121
For You, Mother!	122
Friendship	123
Happy Father's Day	124
Happy Mother's Day!	125
Happy New Year!	126
It's Your Day, Mom!	127
My Sunshine!	128
New Year, Come!	129
Thank You!	130
To A Special Sister!	131
Epilogue	132
About the Author	133

Section – I
Encouragement

A Jewel

Sometimes in life it seems you find,
A jewel rich and rare-
Its beauty, depth and constant shine,
Deem more than you can bear!

You want to hold it close to you,
And yet you know its gleam
Must not be hid, but put in view
So others see its beam!

It's like the pearl that one man found,
Its value was so great-
He sold his all to buy the ground,
Where this pearl lay in wait!

This poem is a parallel
Of truth I hope you see-
For Jesus is this jewel rare,
He waits for you and me!

He wants to shine through us each day,
In word or song or deed-
To show the lost He is the way,
Fulfilling every need!

A Journey

This thing's a journey we call life,
Sometimes it's joy, sometimes it's strife-
Sometimes it's mountains oh so high,
But then it's valleys, where we cry!

God planned this journey for all men,
To bring us back to Him again-
That's why the valley's fixed between
The mountains high, to be unseen!

Yes, in the valley is where God
So many times will let us trod-
For in the valley He restores
The soul of those whom He adores!

Along this journey without doubt,
God teaches us what life's about-
For many great and noble men
Have found their way to God again!

So make your journey be worthwhile,
And bring to all your world a smile-
For truly at this journey's end,
Be found as one known as God's friend!

Biding One's Time

Our daily affairs too oft go awry,
Making us wonder what else we should try-
We wonder if life is really worthwhile,
If biding one's time will last one more mile!

One writer declares we struggle within,
Flesh against spirit to see who will win-
Yet somehow the 'will' continues to strive,
Encouraging self to not lose its drive!

Now what does biding one's time really mean?
Awaiting each day, enduring, serene-
Knowing that this too will not always last,
Trusting the future will outweigh the past!

If viewed in this light we know beyond doubt,
To bide is a time that God's all about-
Waiting is part of God's ultimate plan,
For in this domain He can speak to man!

So do not complain when life takes a turn,
Reason is, we may have something to learn-
Our God's in control and He'll see us through,
'Cause biding one's time can help to imbue!

Character

How long have you been on top of the mount?
Not long enough, you say-
For the mountaintop is where blessings count
Fulfill my needs each day!

Not so, says the One, who stands high above
And knows you inside out-
In the valley is where you let Me, love,
Build character, no doubt!

For your character's like that little song
The kids sing, 'Deep and wide'-
Producing deep character makes you strong,
And there's no need to hide!

Yet you say, not me, I wanna stand tall,
And wave my banner high-
But character says I'll bow to the call,
And serve You 'til I die!

Does character mean what it should to you?
Or do you really care?
God's character builds a life that is true,
And gives you more to share!

Choices

The Story of Samson, Judges chs. 13-16!

There once was a man in the Bible we're told,
Whose birth was a gift to parents of old-
God said He would give this one who would be
A Nazarite-strength and virility!

He grew in wisdom but in his heart still,
A struggle pursued to conquer his will-
His weakness was strong and as he gave in,
He found himself wrapped in bondage to sin!

Because he allowed the flesh free reprise,
The enemy conquered and put out his eyes!
They made him the laughing stock of the crowd,
Sneering and jeering and scoffing aloud!

Yet there in the midst he found in his heart
A place to repent, and ask God to start
Forgiveness anew to him so that he,
Might prove what again he truly could be!

So there in the end he conquered his foe,
With strength from above, his power to show,
He died with them all to prove just the same,
That even in death true life he would gain!

Come Walk with Me

'Come, take my hand and walk with Me,
I'll bring to pass things you can't see-
Your life is Mine, so let us go,
There's new dimensions yet to know!'

He spoke these words in voice so kind,
They brought to me such peace of mind-
Why should I fear, He knows the way,
Assuredly He'll be my stay!

To walk with God and trust His care,
Is life that only few will dare
Allow to happen, for it seems
His ways are not always our dreams!

We want our cake and eat it too,
And boast about the things we do-
Yet, how about the sinner still?
Does he inflict upon our will?

We must submit and let our God,
Direct the paths that we now trod-
With hand in hand let's walk and sing,
While watching our God do great things!

COME WALK WITH ME, SAYS GOD!

Focus

Focus your vision on things that are near,
Focus your hearing on things that are clear-
Focus your thinking on things that are pure-
Focus your doing on people in need!

Why should you focus so much in this life?
Focus will keep you from living in strife-
Each time you focus your heart will be sure,
That someone close by could use a good deed!

Too many people live life at its best
Fulfilling themselves, forget all the rest-
Life is too short to be worried, they say,
With those who probably just need a friend!

Jesus was focused for all of mankind,
To give of Himself, He never did mind-
His perfect example is still good today,
And He'll keep us focused until the end!

Folks!

Almaleen, I'll never forget you
Nor this one statement you said!

A dear friend of mine once said with a whim,
'Ain't nothin' like folks except more of them'!
The older I get the more this seems true,
You just never know what some folks will do!

As long as the game of life goes their way,
They'll do all they can to get you to play-
For some folks, you see, must be in control,
To rule their circle of life is their goal!

Of course, this may seem to work for a while,
And when you adhere it brings them a smile-
But later as time unfolds and you tire
Of being controlled, you're then in the fire!

The rulers begin to change their appeal,
So there through the farce you see what is real-
From ruling to ruin so swift turns the tide,
It suddenly seems no one's on your side!

Just live in the now and always beware,
Folks may let you down but God is still there-
Your game of life can be won if you're true,
Allow only God to lord over you!

God's Majesty

The beauty of an Autumn day,
A friendly smile that comes our way-
The coolness from a gentle breeze,
My God above makes all of these!

The chirping of the birds alone
Will bring to any heart a song-
Because it's God who freely gives
To everything the breath to live!

All good and perfect gifts we know
Come down from God, who loves us so-
His love is warmth that flows within
A heart that's cleansed from inbred sin.

So just to know God's majesty
Is in the good things we can see-
He'll lift the soul from deep despair
And bring real joy beyond compare!

Guard Your Heart

Even in the midst of menial chores,
We sense that our heart desires open doors-
For out of it come the issues of life,
And many of which we find will be rife!

Sometimes it behooves the wisest of men,
To hold up the shield again and again-
For even though sin begins in the mind,
It seeks open doors in the heart to find!

So comes this resolve, to take extra care,
We must guard our heart or sin will be there-
It may not seem wrong, perhaps may not be,
But given some time the root makes a tree!

We must look ahead to conquer our foe,
For wars are not won unless we bestow
Our all to the task of winning the race,
The ultimate goal is seeing God's face!

Now we make the choice if we will subdue,
This enemy of our heart and be true-
With quickness we fight and it won't be long,
By guarding our heart again we'll be strong!

His Plan

'You never seem to mind when trials come,'
She smiled and asked, 'Why should I be afraid?
The One who walks with me will keep me brave.'
He answered, 'Yes, and lead you safely home.'

'You never turn your smiles into a frown,'
She spoke with softness, 'That's because of He
Who was so happy and yes, so carefree,
Took up a cross that I might wear a crown!'

'You always think beyond yourself each day,'
She nodded, 'Yes, He showed me how to live,
By His example I know how to give...
For servanthood is truly God's own way!'

'You seem to find such joy in daily life,'
'For sure', she answered, 'joy comes from above,
And joy is evidence of His great love,
The love that conquers fear and doubt and strife!'

'You seem to know much more than mortal man,
Possessing attributes that do impart
A change has come deep down within your heart;'
'Oh yes, indeed, the purpose of His plan!'

It Matters Not

It matters not where you have been,
It matters not at all-
What matters is not where, but when
Will you accept the call?

God's blessed your life abundantly,
So many times you failed-
But you would rise with fervency
To prove your faith prevailed!

It matters not what others say
Or even think of you-
For in the midst God makes a way
To bring His will in view!

So set your face just like a flint,
And let His fire ignite
Within your soul a mighty glint,
That makes the darkness bright!

Your walk with God will then impart
His life in such a way-
There'll be no question when to start
Your call to serve each day!

It's a Setup!

A reminder to my son, from God!

It's a setup! The words did come
Into the young man's mind-
And though they seemed as nil to some
They came as words of kind!

For God speaks oft into the heart
Of this young man, you see-
The reason being to impart
His will and plans to be!

Though God sees now, He also views
The future for us all-
And we can know that which ensues
Will consummate the call!

'You're somewhere in the future and
You look much better than
You look right now, so take a stand;
Kneel down, and be a man!'

These words God spoke, He'll bring to pass,
His purpose will unfold-
This setup may appear as crass,
But in due time, pure gold!

Just 'Round the Bend

While driving toward home I looked to the sky
Amazed at the beautiful view-
The sun shone so bright amid the thin clouds
Reflecting perfection so true!
On the horizon dark clouds hovered low,
The wind and the rain seemed so near-
That which seemed perfect was taken away,
And in its place nothing was clear!
Then suddenly God reminded me, 'Child,
In spite of these contrasts please know-
I have your world in the palm of My hand
No matter what may come or go...
You must remember that life is unsure,
Change-an inevitable thing-
But your God in Heaven is always the same,
So through life to Me you must cling.'
It doesn't matter if sunshine or rain
Affects our lives daily, my friend-
We must determine to hold onto God,
Heaven waits, just 'round the bend!

Letting Go

It seems there are times when life is so cool,
But other times life can be very cruel-
Whichever the case, it's human, you see,
To do what we can to keep harmony!

We fix this and that, and put on a smile,
Yet knowing our hearts are sad all the while-
We pray and confess, believe beyond doubt
That given some time God will work it out!

We fear that our faith may not see us through,
And having done all, what else can we do?
God gives some relief, and so we hold on,
Just waiting until the problem is gone!

Alas! From above, a voice that we know,
Speaks firmly and says, 'Don't hold, just let go'-
For when we let go, we give God free reign
To work in our lives, removing the pain!

Accept letting go as part of God's plan,
Be real with ourselves, as only we can-
Solutions will come and then we will know,
The best thing that we could do was 'let go'!

Mercy

His mercy endures forever,
His grace is bottomless, too-
His love exhausts? No never,
He constantly reaches for you!

To our God of gods, give thanks,
The great Psalmist David cries-
His mercy endures forever,
Our blessing within Him lies!

His mercy is new every morning,
His grace like the morning dew-
His love never deems a warning,
Its floodgates are open to you!

Where would we be without mercy?
How could we live without grace?
What would we do without God's love,
In striving to win this race?

Woe to the man without mercy,
His life truly lived in vain-
For without God's mercy and grace
True life he never will gain!

Moorings

I can only imagine how the ship stood still,
There amidst the waves, helmsman at the wheel…
Just to watch it sway, ropes secured and taut,
Yet it bravely stood, though it seemed for naught.

Somehow from within thoughts began to flow,
'Yes, you're like this ship, much more than you know-
For your moorings here keep you in one place,
And you have no clue what's beyond your space!'

As my mind reached out, there the picture came,
The helmsman was me, and I bowed in shame…
'What more can I do?' came the question sweet,
With my hands outstretched, I stood to my feet!

'Cut the ropes', He said, 'turn your moorings loose,
There's no place for fear, do not act obtuse-
With Me by your side, there's no limit, dear,
What can come to pass, if you'll only hear!'

Moorings aren't for those who will dare to be
Like a ship when it sets its sails for sea…
Once within that realm you will have new sight,
Your freedom will make all the wrong things right!

Once Again

Once again the trials come to sway my faith and view,
Once again the doubts arise and life seems without clue-
Even though the truth prevails and ultimately I know,
I'll walk the straight and narrow path; now which way do I go?

The night is dark and on this trail seems I am all alone,
Yet deep within my heart I know Your presence's never gone-
But once again it seems the load is more than I can bear,
And then within the darkness You say, "Cast on Me your care".

Once again I'm reassured this too shall pass away,
If somehow I will not depend on flesh as arm of stay-
For in the midst of trials, doubts and loneliness I find,
Your faithfulness will bring to me the needed peace of mind!

So once again I lay myself prostrate before you now,
Seeking your forgiveness, tender mercies shown somehow-
For greater is the need of You than is the need of me,
I lay it all down at your feet again to be set free!

Once again let faith arise and bring about Your peace,
For when Your peace prevails all doubts and sorrows have to cease
You are the great I AM and with you all things can be done,
Soon once again I'll walk in light, the light of Your dear Son!

Seasons of Life

Our lives are like the seasons,
They change as time goes by-
Childhood, youth, mid-life, old age,
Don't question how or why.

Childhood's like the springtime,
Everything's so new-
Time really has no essence,
There's much to learn and do!

Youth are full of vigor,
Like summer, filled with haste-
With fun and games and chores galore,
There's just no time to waste!

Then mid-life slips upon us,
So suddenly, from where?
The kids are gone, where's all the fuss?
This time is hard to bear!

Around the corner comes old age,
As time comes to an end-
Upon this earth, our life is o'er,
Eternity waits, my friend!

The Lighthouse

The sea is black, the waters rage, the ship is tossed about,
The helmsman cannot hold the wheel; this is the end no doubt!
The shipmates talk among themselves and finally agree,
The time to call on God is now and humbly bow their knee.
So to the center of the ship they gather in a crowd,
And ask their faithful Captain if he'll lead a prayer aloud.
A sadder scene you'll never see, for all their hope is lost,
Down with the ship they'll bravely go, no matter what the cost!
But suddenly the helmsman shouts and says, 'Friends, have no fear,
I see the lighthouse, we are saved, have faith for land is near!'
And so it is with us today, we sail away from shore,
We think that all is well and life will go on as before.
Life's storms arise, our ship is tossed, and we lose sight of land,
Then suddenly we realize our life is out of hand!
Within ourselves we know there's nothing left for us to do,
Except to call on God and hope His lighthouse will come through.
So, just before we sink we see our stalwart Lighthouse shine;
Jesus is our Lighthouse, and He's always right on time!

The Spicer of Life

Some say variety makes this life sweet,
Others think being alike is so neat-
Whatever brings us to this point of view,
Let it be said that this one thing is true!

One thing is notable and I am sure,
The Spicer of Life will always endure-
Here blah and humdrum just can't stand the test,
Spicer of Life will surpass all the rest!

The lighter side sees the reason for grief,
Knowing the Spicer of Life brings relief-
For no matter what the season we're in,
With Spicer of Life we surely will win!

So look all you want in each avenue,
Somehow remember this truth about you-
You will decide if your life's filled with woe,
You will decide down which road you will go!

The Spicer of Life is waiting each day,
With His arms outstretched and wanting to say,
'Come walk with Me and your life will be new,
There's joy unspeakable waiting for you!'

Until...

A song of old says 'Until then...'
Yes, until goes from way back when
And doesn't stop 'til God says so-
For until lets God's purpose flow!

Keep going, though transition seems
To be afar, in distant dreams-
For change must come, yet disarray
Precedes the goal that God says may
Bring forth His light and future plan,
No will of God through will of man!
Until will break the yoke of sin,
To yield new hope and life within!
And until one stands face to face
With Him who saves us by His grace,
Can until be fulfilled complete,
No, until we bow at His feet...

So never cease to watch and pray,
For surely there will come a day-
We'll understand it better when;
But as for now, it's until then...

Words!

They're in my head, words someone said,
Some harsh and rude, seem to intrude-
My inner man can't understand,
Until the Paraclete I meet-
This One the Son said would come near,
His words to comfort and to cheer!
How powerful His words I've heard,
About my loins He says to gird
The truth, He speaks as does a friend,
To understand and comprehend,
The paraleipsis of the phrase,
Power from the Ancient of Days!
Yes, He will give the will to live,
His power to feed our innermost need.
And only when we bow will He
Come by our side to help us see
Within ourselves we're yet so small,
But by His Spirit we stand tall.
And words we speak that have His touch,
Will go forth fruitful, bearing much!
WORDS!

Section – II
Family

A Man after God's Heart

Written for my son, Josh, a man after God's heart!

David was a shepherd boy before he was a king,
Out in the fields with just the sheep he'd play his harp and sing!
He'd write the Psalms and gladly lift them up before the Lord,
God found them so important that He gave them as His Word!
And that they are, for God alone inspired the young man's thoughts,
He showed to David how his life could be lived as it ought!

From shepherd boy to warrior, fear held no place in him,
He killed a lion and a bear as if a passing whim!
And then one day a giant named Goliath came his way,
So David, with his sling and stone, brought death to him that day!

As he became a man, he found that life was not so fair,
Sin found its way into his mind and to his heart from there-
The consequence was great and David thought that all was lost,
But time revealed through circumstance just how much it would cost!

Alas! This shepherd boy, now king, repents to God above!
He cries aloud for mercy, restoration, joy and love!
And you know what? God gave to him these attributes anew,
Just as He will today for those who need the same things, too!
It matters not what you have done or where you've been before,
The blood of Christ and love of God can satisfy you more!

If you don't know this story that I share with you today,
You'll find it in the Bible where God put it just to say-
If you desire to be a person after God's own heart,
Beware, for sin will come your way to see if you'll depart!

Pursuing God is not an easy task to undertake,
So just remember your eternal soul will be at stake!
No matter who you are or where you go or what you do,
You need the Lord right by your side, the One who's always true!
Be king or pauper, black or white, the needs are all the same,
Salvation to the heart and soul is free in Jesus' name!

A Walk down Memory Lane

Reflecting upon the years in the past
Brings memories dear, the kind that will last-
For here in the deep recesses of mind
Are faces of those so cherished through time.

Irene was my aunt who fervently prayed,
Instilling in me a fact that has stayed-
She trusted in God as Saviour and Guide,
Her faith was in bloom the day that she died!

Velma and Sissy, Ruth and Tommie Lou,
These dear aunts of mine now with Jesus, too!
They stayed true and faithful, never gave in
To that which they knew would cultivate sin!

Their dear sister, Bess, the baby, still lives,
She too loves the Lord, and constantly gives
Her life to her family whom she loves so,
A heritage true she'll leave when she goes!

So once in a while walk down memory lane,
And let yourself know just how much you gain
By having kinfolk whose love still lives on,
In spite of the fact that they may be gone!

Be Thankful!

I have a mother ninety-three
Who, everyday, still teaches me-
Be thankful!
Yes, surely thankfulness is rare,
For nowdays it seems most care
Is focused on the person ME,
So not too many people see-
Be thankful!

Feed the hungry, meet a need
For some poor soul astray
Be thankful to forego a deed
That just might change their day!

It never hurts to be so kind
And strive to have a Christlike mind
For showing forth this attribute
You manifest the Spirit's fruit-
Be thankful!

Don't ever let a day go by,
That you don't hesitate to try
To show your world the reason why
You're thankful!

Family Life

In Honor of my 93 year old daddy,
Milledge Mullis, who departed this life, 5/7/07

Just look at his hands, they tell of his work,
It's something he loved and never did shirk-
Daylight would find him afar down the road,
Already prepared to buy a big load!

Radiators, batt'ries, aluminum too,
Copper his favorite, yes all these will do-
Sometimes he would have pecans to the end,
But no matter what, he's "Junk" to his friends!

Back home in the kitchen you'd find mama dear,
Always in her apron and full of good cheer-
Cooking and cleaning 'most times with a song,
These chores made her happy all the day long!

She'd look out the window, there with a grin
She'd see daddy coming, truck loaded again-
Supper was ready, it never was late,
For daddy was hungry, no time to wait!

Although there were times when all was not good,
The love that we shared somehow has withstood-
So when we remember the good more than bad,
It now makes me thankful for all that we had!

Freedom

Dedicated to my cousin, Nancy Browning!

It takes fortitude and grit to be strong,
To stand up and fight though it may seem wrong-
But freedom's not cheap, and if you think so,
Then join with the troops and see where you go!

Women and men are now joined hand in hand,
Trying to bring about peace through the land-
So let us focus on teams just like these,
Who willingly give of themselves overseas!

Although they are treading in waters unknown,
They're made aware that they're never alone-
Thanks to someone like my 'cuz, Delta Queen,
Who shares love and smiles, a spirit serene!

Flying with confidence just as she has
For thirty-four years, yes, she's got pizazz!
Brings them God's Word and His love so divine,
Builds comradery and lets His light shine!

So after these trips to bring the troops home,
Only God knows how much seed has been sown-
Nancy, we laud all your efforts for Him,
And pray that your light will never grow dim!

Kinfolk

Dedicated to my Uncle Leghmon & Aunt Dot,
Who lived down the road!

Here in the country we have kinfolk near,
They live down the road and bring us good cheer!
We laugh and we cry and fuss a lot, too,
But those are just things that all kinfolk do!

Uncle Leghmon, Aunt Dot, they're quite a pair,
They've been through a lot, but love is still there-
Two girls and three boys they raised through hard times,
Now these try to make their life more sublime!

My unc lost a leg which caused lots of strife,
A boar hog with tusks almost took his life-
He lost all his blood, stared death in the face,
But God wasn't ready, He gave him more grace!

Aunt had to work hard to help them adjust,
To get through hard times they found were a must-
Yet God has become more dear to them now,
He proved that His love was greater somehow!

It takes good and bad to make life complete,
Nothing's so bitter it can't be made sweet-
Aunt Dot, Uncle Leghmon, hope by now you know,
As kinfolk of ours, we sure love you so!

My Heritage

In honor of my wonderful parents,
Milledge & Thelma Mullis

When I was a child, for reasons unknown,
My birth parents moved and left me alone-
Out in the country, away from the fold,
An elderly lady my keeper, I'm told.

It seemed no one cared, except God of course,
Who knew all along there'd be no remorse-
For He would provide a mom and dad dear,
To adopt me in love and always be near!

They taught me about unconditional love,
The kind that can only come down from above-
It stands and forbears when all is at loss,
And never gives up, no matter the cost!

Now half a century has gone and I should
Relate in this story that all is still good-
They've grown old in age, are nearing the end,
But always will know they've been my godsend!

My heritage great is important to me,
For I was born, then 'chosen', you see-
A life that was bleak, by God was made glad,
Because of my wonderful mother and dad!

My Mama

In honor of Thelma Mullis, my precious Mama,
now 93, who has grown old gracefully!

Her sister, Irene, had six girls and a boy,
And all of them brought to mama much joy-
Although she had none of her own it seemed
To hold her own little one was her dream!

One day she and daddy received an ad
Of a child in need of a mom and dad-
Though this little girl was eighteen months old,
She was still small enough to hug and hold!

Adoption became their ultimate choice,
At last they would have a wee little voice
Calling them 'mama and diddy' each day,
Bringing fulfillment of fam'ly their way!

Mama's dream had come true, she had her own
Little one to teach until she was grown-
About love and life and how to trust God,
That fam'ly was there where ever she trod!

It's been fifty years and Mama still knows
This 'baby' of hers has strived to bestow
Upon her and daddy the love they shared,
And show 'til the end just how much she cared!

My Uncle-The Barber

Dedicated to daddy's brother, Walter,
Who is 96 years old now!

He fishes and hunts, has a garden and goats,
And somehow he never did sow his wild oats!
For years he was known as the barber in town,
That was the place where the men hung around!

His prices were cheap, he did a good job,
So usu'lly he'd have a pretty good mob-
They'd chew and they'd spit and argue awhile,
But most of the time they left wid a smile!

Now he's ninety-two, aunt Lois is gone,
She lingered awhile, but God called her home-
Three girls and three boys all visit quite much,
And make sure they always give him a touch!

Each Sunday will find him driving to church,
And once in a while he might even lurch-
But he doesn't care, that's part of old age,
It's certainly not what some call road rage!

Uncle Walter, the barber, farmer and friend,
You've been through a lot and now near the end-
You've lived a full life, continue to trust
In Christ as your Saviour, Heaven's a must!

My Uncle-The Preacher

Dedicated to mama's baby brother, Cullen,
Who is dear to us all!

He found the Lord dear when he was a lad,
Salvation was his and my, was he glad!
The burden was lifted, he saw the light,
And God spoke a call to his heart one night!

His zeal and his passion for God ran deep,
His heart was so full, at times he would weep-
Seeking the Lord every day for a song,
He knew that with God, he'd never go wrong!

He'd go to the woods and preach to the birds,
Such singin' and preachin' you never have heard-
He'd pray and he'd cry, and talk to the Lord,
Constantly searching for truth in the Word!

The years have gone by and he's ministered much
To souls near and far, he's seen the Lord touch-
He's married and buried and baptized his share,
Given his all just to show of his care!

My uncle, the preacher, Cullen's his name,
He's proven that life is never the same
When someone will yield to God and be true,
Faith will abound, God's love will shine through!

The Love of a Son

Dedicated to my son, Josh,
Who means the world to me!

I'm sure you have heard this adage of old,
Perhaps for you some truth it may hold-
'A daughter's a daughter all of her life,
A son's a son 'til he gets him a wife.'

Well, I have an only child who's a son,
So until he gets a wife, he's just one-
Then in their union, the one becomes two,
And to each other their love should stand true.

The love they share is not like another,
So is the love of the son and mother-
For the heart has rooms big enough to share,
When the bond for the family is there!

The mother-in-law must not be a threat,
But rather should be to both an asset-
No matter the mood nor time they will know
Her home is a place where either can go.

The love of a son should never wax cold,
But grow through the years as mother grows old-
He'll never regret the bonds in this life
That only he shares with his mother and wife!

The Shop

In honor of "Chasers" Expresso,
Our 1st Christian Coffeeshop!

It all began because the son
Had vision to believe
That God could bring the shop to pass,
His purpose He would weave!

The townsfolk only made a joke
Out of the old 'rattrap'-
What good could come from something new?
God sought one for the gap!

At first it seemed that all was good,
That maybe it would work-
God drew some in from near and far,
Yet even church folk shirked!

The coffee shop was planned by God,
A funnel, if you will-
To pour His presence into lives
That did not know Him still!

And even now there yet remains
Those whom the townsfolk shun-
So God will choose another route,
To see His great work done!

Three Wishes

Inspired by my son, Josh, still 'chasing'

I call this young man a 'chaser' indeed,
His heart had a plan to help those in need-
A youth group he made by God's help, no doubt,
This first wish God gave showed what faith's about!

In wisdom he grew, his spirit was meek,
Yet he always knew his flesh would be weak-
So closer to God he strived to remain,
The path he would trod will be full of change!

His heart again felt there's no place to stop,
This second wish dealt with the need for a shop-
A coffee shop, yes, a gift from above,
God used as a tool to show forth His love!

Then after a while the young man so yearned
To travel a mile with one who was learned-
A man of God true took him down a road,
And taught what he knew to lighten his load!

This third wish God used to somehow instill
His various views into 'chaser's' will-
Three wishes have now enlarged this young man,
So onward he trods, pursuing God's plan!

Section – III
Friends

As I Go!

Josh Parham (SpideyMan)!
Dewitt, it seems so apropos
To get my mom to write
This poem to you as I go
In faith, to do what's right!

You'll never know how much it meant,
To have you as my boss
Our crossing paths was heaven sent,
So let's not count it loss!

Your friendly smile, a nightly sign,
Displayed your feelings well
For you were never mean, just kind,
And anyone could tell!

Your words of affirmation came,
Each time the job was done
And to us all, you were the same,
Commending everyone!

So 'thank you' for allowing me,
To serve FEDEX with you
Perhaps some soul there soon shall see,
That Jesus loves them, too!

As You Marry

Dear Jason and Beth, this poem's for you,
Wishing you blessings as you say 'I do'-
You'll find new meaning as you begin life,
Walking together, as husband and wife.

Not only as spouse, but best friend as well,
Giving your all, leaving nothing to tell-
Sharing those moments expressing your heart,
Bonding together your love from the start!

There may be days when it seems life's not fair,
Those are the times that you really must care-
Never let selfish ambition and pride
Take precedence o'er what you feel inside!

Always remember that God is supreme,
Let Him be center of all of your dreams-
If He is sovereign in your lives each day,
Blessings and honor He'll send forth your way!

Now as you marry, may love, joy and peace,
Daily be attributes that will increase-
And may this union be blessed from above,
Granting your home always be full of love!

'Becca Jane

For the birth of Rebecca Jane,
Firstborn of Kelly & Brad Davis

We all remember the cute little rhyme,
That tells of a life of love so sublime!
'In love, then marriage, and then a surprise,
The news that a baby's growing inside'!

So is the tale for this twosome we know,
A little one dear whose face will soon show-
Of course, 'Papa Mimmie' decides on a name,
To go with Rebecca, it's gotta be Jane!

Jane is 'MemMe Donna's' middle name, too,
So Kelly and Brad say, OK, will do-
Now 'Becca Jane is the first one in line,
To carry 'French-Davis' throughout all time!

This happy event will bring joy and tears,
Not only today, but down through the years-
She'll be Number 1, rule the heart of dad, Brad,
'Papa Ray', 'NanNa Carol', will also be glad!

Mom Kelly, of course, along with the rest,
Will do all she can to give her the best-
Here's wishing Godspeed and blessings galore,
For this little one whom they all will adore!

Covenant Brothers

Dedicated to Josh and Bryan, Godchasers!

While seeking the Lord for opportune grand,
God granted a wish come true by His hand-
And in due process He added a friend,
Covenants brothers, we'll be 'til the end!

For truly we share a bond of pursuit,
To chase after God and show forth His fruit-
Our crossing of paths was not happenstance,
God granted to both of us a new chance!

To see if indeed the heart could be pure,
Along with clean hands to do His work sure-
If so, then to stand in His holy place,
Daily be filled with unwavering grace!

As time marches on, may we so be found
Doing His bidding on unfertile ground-
Unfeigned in our labors, sowing His seed,
Showing His light to a dark world in need!

So covenant brothers, take a stand now,
No time to turn back, just hold to the plow-
Follow the leader, yes trust and obey,
This could be the dawn of a brand new day!

Growing Old

Dedicated to those who take care of my folks!

Life's full of changes, somehow, we are told,
Through process of time, we die or grow old-
We just never know what may lie ahead,
For life growing old can bring fear or dread!

It seems there are some who truly are blessed,
To stay in their home and find quiet rest-
But others demand assistance and cheer,
'Westview Rehab' we're so glad that you're here!

Just walk down the halls, it doesn't take long,
You may hear a cry, you may hear a song-
You may meet someone who seems quite aloof,
Or maybe there's one you know who's obtuse!

Some of the folk are not able to walk,
And others as well, who just cannot talk-
But there's quite a few who've accepted the trends,
Wheelchairs and walkers are now their best friends!

Each day all the Staff show love and concern,
For here in this place, there's so much to learn
About growing old, yes, one day, you see,
The ones growing old here may be you and me!

Happy 30th Anniversary!

Written for Jean at Dublinair,
For her anniversary!

Thirty years have come and gone
It seems but yesterday-
I gave my heart to you alone,
And wanted it that way!

You truly are my soulmate, love,
Without you I'd be lost-
I daily thank my God above,
He helps us count the cost!

Life's not been fair to us at times,
Yet love sustains us still-
For soulmates never cease to share
And lay aside self-will!

Your gentleness with mother dear,
Yes, now her sister, too-
And with the kids you make it clear,
The love that dwells in you!

So on our anniversary
May it not go untold-
It's me for you, and you for me,
Together, let's grow old!

Happy 50th Anniversary, Almaleen & Billy!

It seems like only yesterday
When you first said "I do",
You pledged your love in every way
And promised to be true!

The years went by and God saw fit
To give to you two boys-
Through them you never lost your wit,
For they have been your joys!

You worked and never gave a thought
What else the Lord might send-
But later years with their lives wrought
Your two then turned to ten!

Retirement came for both of you
Some sickness ran its course-
But life together still was true
No need to have remorse!

Now 50 years have come and gone
And you're together still-
The love you pledged has merely grown
As God enlarged the wheel!

Rejoice, this special day is here
For you to celebrate-
God's blessed your union with good cheer
And lots more on the wait!

July 4th, 2003

Happy 50th Anniversary, Ellen & Don!

It seems like only yesterday
When you first said, 'I do'-
You pledged your love in every way
And promised to be true!

You both worked hard, it was a time
You laughed and then you cried-
But all in all, life was sublime,
As you walked, 'side by side'!

And then one day God sent to you
A precious baby boy-
This one named Scott you vowed would do,
He's still your pride and joy!

Then Scott and Amy made life great!
Catherine came, you see -
This one was truly worth the wait,
She's grand, as grands can be!

Now fifty years have come and gone,
So celebrate today-
And know that all the love you've shown
Will never pass away!

February 2, 2008

Happy 50th Birthday, Brenda!

Dedicated to one of my 'bestest' friends!

Another milestone has been reached and my, how blessed you are!
To say that you are fifty now gives clout unknown thus far-
For you have now arrived in what is known to all mid-life,
The circle that revolves around you constantly is rife!

Experience from trial and error takes a different turn,
For been there, done that now is past, so much you've had to learn!
It's wonderful to see someone who's been so kind and true,
To God & family, friends & foe, your love always shines through.

Yes, mom and dad were blessed the day you came into their world,
And tho' the times were tough you've always let your faith unfurl-
For you intended to make life be just as full and free,
As David who said, 'My heart follows hard, God, after thee!'

So life or something like it is the saying for today,
It starts with birth and ends at death, not really, so you say-
For surely there's a God above who has prepared a place
In Heaven just for those He saved and kept in life through grace.

We hail you, Brenda, and we wish you all the best God has,
And even when the times seem blah, just know God sends pizzazz!
He's brought you where you are today and surely you'll be fine
In mid-life, fifty years is nifty, let your love light shine!

Happy 60ᵗʰ Birthday, Pastor!

Dedicated to my Pastor, David Stanton,
A Prince of a fellow!

On special days we reminisce of good ole days gone by,
We major on the ones of bliss and minor on goodbyes-
Reflecting back for sixty years, I'm sure that you'll agree,
Tho' many times you had your fears, you knew where faith would be.

God called you to His service and equipped you as you gave
Your all to Him and took a stand to see the lost ones saved-
He gave a helpmate and a friend to be there by your side,
She'd be your lover 'til the end, one you'd protect and guide!

And through this union God saw fit to send you children three,
One girl, two boys, made of true grit just as PKs should be!
Altho' they're grown and now you have a grandson one year old,
This season of your life will change to stories yet untold!

So just remember this cliché and rise above the tide,
Not older yet but wiser still, and deeper more than wide-
For God has fashioned in your heart abilities yet sure,
No matter age or come what may, 'clean hands & heart that's pure'.

God bless you, Pastor, as you reach this milestone in your life,
Anointing greater than you've known and peace when there is strife-
Yes, may you know you're greatly loved by all who march with you,
And God's success will lie ahead, 'to thine own heart be true'!

Happy 90th Birthday!

Written for my friend, Patti Walden's mother,
Mrs. Thelma Farmer, who departed this life
8/21/07, at the age of 93!

Another year has come and gone,
It's birthday time again-
And mother dear, you've always shone
Your love since way back when!

Altho' you've reached this grand milestone
Of ninety years with pride-
The twinkle in your eyes has shone
There's still much love inside!

You may not seem to be aware
Of who I am or why
Your home is now at Dublinair,
Sure, in the past you'd cry!

But mother dear, I feel your love
And never will I cease
Each day to ask the Lord above
To grant comfort and peace!

So this is just a little way
To show how much I care-
And when God calls you home someday,
Wait for me, I'll be there!

Medicine Lady

Written to my friend, Jennifer Margopolus, PA
With John D. Northup, MD

She wears a white coat and works everyday,
Leaves no room for doubt that she's a PA-
Ambition and zeal combined with her care,
Are attributes she does willingly share!

I call her 'Medicine Lady' for sure,
Because her desire is seeking a cure-
She's due all respect her patients can give,
For their well being gives reason to live!

She smiles with a gleam you see in her eyes,
Feels empathy with a patient who cries-
Though busy she is, she knows beyond doubt,
Medicine is what her life's all about!

Some say it's a call, not lightly to take,
A rigorous role for much is at stake-
Not much time for self, demands never cease,
So surely the need for God's inner peace!

Yes, Jennifer, life holds so much in store,
As you live and learn like never before-
May you realize the gift you possess
Was given by God to share and to bless!

My Friend

Dedicated to my long time friend, Liesa,
Who inspired this poem-we did it all!

I asked if you would walk with me a mile, you said, 'No, two',
So off we started, hand in hand, we found so much to do!
Adventure filled our days and nights along this friendship way,
To parks and shops and scenic sights, and food galore each day!

Down to the beach, out to the mall, or just to sit and stare
Up at the sky at night to see full moon and stars were there-
Life's so much fun when you can share your time with someone who
Enjoys this life and strives to prove that friendship's still in bloom!

We live in such a fast paced world 'til friendship's almost lost,
So if you find within your realm just one, it's worth the cost-
You are that one, my friend indeed, and this is sent from me
As but a small reminder of just what a friend should be!

Tho' time has passed, we're older now, yet still I see those miles,
And each time that I reminisce, it brings to me such smiles-
For life was meant to be a time to share with someone dear,
If for a season, or a reason, whether far or near!

Don't ever feel like you're alone now that you're far away,
You'll always be dear to my heart through each and every day-
I love you and appreciate the fact that you and I
Will share this bond of friendship, yes, until the day I die!

Noah!

Written for my friend, Margie's, grandson,
For his 4th birthday—quite a little man!

He's only four years old and yet
He seems to be so grown-
A finer son you've never met,
No bashfulness he's shown!

He's quite the little man around
The house, at school and play-
His wit and cleverness abound
To all who comes his way!

Yes, Amie Chan, you two are blessed,
To have this precious son-
And even tho' some days seem stressed,
He's there when day is done!

Noah, the name means 'rest and peace,
Strong, slow and loyal friend'-
And as he grows may he increase
In wisdom with no end!

Noah, to thine own self be true,
As in this life you grow-
Never doubt that 'Jesus loves you,
The Bible tells you so'.

Persevere!

Written at the request of LouAnn New,
A friend, while she was in ICU!

Love, peace and joy! Our great God will employ,
For even in our trials, yes all the devil's wiles
Are but a passing fad, soon sorrow will be glad,
And all our hue and cry will vanish by and by!

We serve the One who stills the gales of life at will,
He never will digress nor lose His sweet caress-
For those who know this One will stand when day is done
And shout the victory for all the world to see!

Don't ever lose your hope for then in life you grope
As one who's in the dark, and knows he can't embark
Upon his ship of dreams, for yielding to the schemes
Has made his spirit sad, which once was free and glad!

Yes, trials come and go, and just to let you know
That once you pass this test, a glimmer of the best
Will shine within your world, as faith again unfurls
And brings you to a place with His so matchless grace!

Love, joy and peace, for sure these do not cease,
And while you persevere, know He is standing near
With answers on the way, yes, even for this day,
And in a little while, you'll walk the last long mile!

Tell Him Who You Are

Inspired by book written by my boss,
John D. Northup, MD

Tell him who you are from the very start,
Tell him who you are, share with him your heart-
Do not be afraid, help him understand,
If your need is great don't withhold your hand.

Love will be the bond, yes it is the key,
Don't assume he knows what his eyes can't see-
Let him be a friend who can penetrate
Any kind of wall that might separate.

All too many times life will not be fair,
So you need someone who will not despair-
As a dear helpmate he has come your way,
To be there for you as your chief mainstay!

You will never know what life holds for you,
If you never share your own point of view-
If true love abounds, you will rightly know
He is there for you, he will help you grow!

Tell him who you are, never make him guess,
Let him know your need of his dear caress-
Life on earth is short but it can be sweet,
Tell him who you are, make his life complete!

Thank You-Our Seniors!

A Tribute to all of our Christian Senior Citizens!

We want you to know the investments you made
In the past are still vital for all us today-
You weathered the storms of life, now it seems
There's not a lot left to fulfill your dreams!

But you still impact the lives that you touch
By being just you, and giving so much-
We look to your strength and confidence true
Praying, 'God, grant us these attributes, too!'

For only God knows what you took to be tough
And keep going on when times were so rough-
You took up your cross and bore it each day,
You trusted in God, so let come what may!

We hold you in high regard and esteem
You here in the church, you're part of God's team!
Your prayers and your love we need 'til the end,
You're one in a million on whom we depend!

So even though life is winding on down,
Your hope still remains one day in your crown-
For Heaven is real, and so is God's Son,
You will be rewarded for good that you've done!

The Blind Lady

Dedicated to the blind lady at
Richmond County Courthouse,
Augusta, Ga.

Today I saw a sight that made me weep,
For all too often we think life is cheap-
But there within her store she bravely stood,
A woman blind, yet striving to do good!

Her task would seem so menial to some,
Yet she must demonstrate great strength to come-
Not physical, but in her 'will' she sees
This tiny possibility to please!

I'm sure at first she had to battle fear,
Fear of rejection; not knowing who is near-
And what if, at this job she can't succeed
By selling goods that other folks might need?

So when we entered I asked God above
To gently touch her heart with His great love-
And keep her safe within the courthouse walls,
Each day that passes as she heeds her call.

Her handicap is now her cross to bear,
But God, no doubt, is totally aware-
And if within her heart His loves abides,
Then one day she will see Him 'eye to eye'!

The Godchaser

Dedicated to Rev. Tommy & Jeannie Tenney,
(The Godchasers) who poured into my son's life!

At times in this life it's good when we meet
With others unknown, and share a time sweet-
The giftings are pure, the knowledge abounds,
'Tis true of this man described as 'profound'!

His simple approach, tho' deep are his words,
Brings message of hope in ways yet unheard-
Worship and unity are his mainstay-
Hunger for more, his incentive to pray!

The Godchaser shares from his heart so deep
The stories of old, that surely we'll weep-
And ask God to change the way that we view
This life day by day in all that we do!

The songs Jeannie sings, her gifting as well,
Hold much truth indeed in all that they tell-
Anointed by God, she gives it her all,
Enhancing this team, fulfilling their call!

Tommy and Jeannie, may you realize
The impact you make on so many lives-
Is changing our world; perhaps one by one
Are now 'Chasing God' until life is done!

The Sisters Three

For Giovanna, Mary, Susie,
And of course, Mom Toni!

For sure, all knew that mom was 'Sarge',
She ruled with force and woe-
And seldom was she not in charge,
With three girls in a row!

She made them learn their abc's
And always go to mass-
There never was much time to tease,
'Mid church and work and class!

The sisters grew to womanhood,
And though change came to life-
Upon the Rock they've firmly stood
As Christian, Mom and Wife!

They're older now, but there's no doubt
The bond of love they share-
Is what real fam'ly love's about,
For each, the other's there!

The 'Sarge'? Oh yes, she's made her mark,
In life, as most moms do-
So may she never be too stark
To whisper, 'I love you'...
TO THE SISTERS THREE!

What Is a Nurse?

Written for an RN on 4th Floor at FPH

'What is a nurse?', the young child did ask,
'Where are they from?, and what is their task?'
The mother replied, 'Just watch and you'll see,
They're from near and far, for you and for me.

A nurse has a heart to help people mend,
No matter the need, the nurse is a friend-
They do their job well and do it with pride,
Because of a call from God deep inside!

Not just anyone can be a nurse, child,
It takes one who strives to be meek and mild-
To care for the one unkempt and unloved,
The nurse will display God's gift from above!

For nursing is God extended to man,
One not afraid, child, to reach forth a hand
To touch your hot brow and whisper a prayer,
That you might know God has you in His care!

So, what is a nurse? Perhaps you now know,
Angels of mercy God sent to bestow
Their ministry gifts each day that they live,
For all those in need, to them freely give!'

Section – IV
Grief

A Tribute to "Bubba"

His name was Conrad Henderson, but "Bubba" to his friends,
To tell of his accomplishments for sure there is no end-
He served his country in Korea, suffered many woes,
Through frostbite, bombings, loss of life of friends as well as foes!

Though short in stature, he stands tall, especially today,
He's crossed the bar, has made it home, for Jesus showed the way-
Yes, "Bubba" made his peace with God before it was too late,
He found God's love could conquer all life's bitterness and hate!

He was no man of many words- he loved his shop where he
Spent many hours making ships that never went to sea-
The workmanship that they display is but a parallel
Of how the hand of God can make a sickened soul be well!

For when he started with a piece of wood that seemed so tough,
Not long within his hands you'd see a shape without a rough-
Yes, he knew how to make it all begin to blend together,
Just as our God whose workmanship with us will last forever!

He loved his wife and daughter dear, the grands, yes they were grand,
And though perhaps he never spoke of love, he was not bland-
His humor always had a way of surfacing somehow
Though dry at times, his wit would show a smile and wrinkled brow!

So on this day may we salute this soldier brave and true,
He never shirked his duties or gave up, as some men do-
May God grant "Bubba's" good deeds done
through life outweigh the bad,
With every loving thought of him as Husband, Grand and Dad!
WE'LL MISS YOU, "BUBBA"...
October 13, 2006

In Memory of 'Curly'

His name was Mathew, but 'Curly' to us,
A man of God, someone you could trust-
He wasn't ashamed to show forth his call,
Was willing to reach out to help one and all!

Although born a Jew, he gave Christ his heart,
And vowed while he lived on earth to impart
The truth that unwavering faith was the key
To living a joyous life, full and free!

He knew the Word well, his memory keen,
Could stand and recite the facts he had gleaned-
His voice was still strong, though winded some days,
Yet he never waned in singing God's praise!

When failing health came, he never gave in
To things that could wage or cultivate sin-
His love for his wife was evident, too,
Portraying that no matter what, he was true!

Yes, Curly is one we'll never forget,
Though not understood by some that he met-
His message rings loud today in this place,
For sure he knew well, God's 'Amazing grace'!
WE'LL MISS YOU, CURLY!
8/19/07

Our Blessed Hope

In memory of my precious Aunt Irene, who
Departed this life 2/17/85!

One night while on my bed I lay,
I saw Aunt Irene and heard her say
These words with such a smile and care,
Confirming she awaits us there!

It seemed she called my name so sweet,
Just as she would each time we'd meet-
Yet different now, because you see,
She's there, not here-immortality!

"Don't weep for me because I'm gone,
I've made it to my brand new home-
Through all the sorrows, trials and tests,
At last my weary soul finds rest!

It's worth it all to be His child,
To make it through the last long mile-
It's worth it all to hear Him say,
'Well done, my child, you're home to stay'!"

So serve Him while you're on life's shore,
For mortal life will soon be o'er-
And when the Reaper calls your name,
You, too, will hear Christ say the same...

"Well done, my child, you've made it through,
The joys of Heaven welcome you-
Christ the Saviour, loved ones so dear,
Waiting is o'er, the family's all here!"

The Door

In memory of cousin, Gloria, who
Departed this life 5/7/05!

While musing upon some precious events,
Of 'Glory' in days that are past-
It seems so unfair how fast they were spent,
Yet thankfully memories last!

Our life must be lived for time does not wait,
And that which we sow we will reap-
Our destiny call will not beckon late,
Death is an appointment we'll keep!

While sitting beside her bed in the dark,
And holding her weak, feeble hand-
My mind's eye did see her ship had embarked,
She peered for that beautiful land!

The door that was shut has now opened wide,
Her pain and her tears are all gone-
Jesus, her Saviour, is right by her side,
Greeting her, 'Child, welcome home!'

Eternity's door will open for all,
Prepare now and do not delay-
Hearken intently, respond to His call,
For Heaven is one breath away!

The Love of God

In memory of Jerred Proctor, Cousin Gwen's son,
Who departed this life 3/17/06 !

Down and dirty, full of lies,
Sniffing, coughing, blood shot eyes-
Nowhere now to go at night,
A borrowed bed, a beggar's plight!

Who really cares? Whose was this child?
A Christian family, meek and mild-
The ones who raised this child to know
The love of God can none outgrow!

When at the altar he would pray,
The love of God would be his stay-
But somewhere on his youthful road,
He found that life became a load.

There on the street the pressures came,
His so called friends, a brand new game-
With truth or dare, the dare would win,
And on its heels a brand new sin!

'Where is his soul?', life here is o'er,
Hell or Heaven, distant shore-
With hope that somehow at the end,
The love of God was still his friend!

What 'Will' It Be?

When sorrow comes and clouds are grey,
There doesn't seem to be a way
To fill the voids that sorrow brings,
Except to search for brand new things.

At first, we have no real desire
To once again allow the fire
Of life and love to burn anew-
We must recant this point of view.

For in the midst of sorrow, friend,
The reason does not bring an end-
But rather something better still,
A fresh beginning of the 'will'.

The 'will' to choose a different road,
To find someone to share the load-
To have a peace of heart and mind,
That nowhere in this world you'll find.

For peace will come from up above,
The God of Heaven, God of love,
Will send it to you now and then,
By way of prayer, by way of friends!

Where Do We Go From Here?

In memory of Ken and Tammy Alligood

'Where do we go from here?' were the thoughts
As they laid their loved ones to rest-
These ones so dear will no longer be heard
For they've reached the end of their quest.

This life here is o'er, eternity waits
Not only for them, but for all-
The ultimate end is not rendered by fate
But by how we answer the call.

Life is a vapor, so soon it will end,
All sickness and sin will be o'er-
Let's keep looking up to Heaven, my friend,
For those who have gone on before.

Reach up to God, let your heart be contrite,
Pour brokenness down at His feet-
Then He will give you a song in the night,
That will make your living complete.

Don't underestimate God and His plans,
He asks you to trust and obey-
Just follow His will and make no demands,
Let His Spirit show you the way.

Section – V
Hope

Alone with God

There's no other place that I'd rather be,
Than alone with God at night by the sea-
The sound of the waves brings a quiet still
To my restless soul in search of God's will!

My life took a turn with uncertainty,
A strange kind of twist had happened to me-
'Abandon' was all the Lord seemed to say,
No clue as to what this word would defray.

For once long ago abandoned I was,
As but a mere child not knowing the cause-
Tho' too young to see or spiritually know
That being alone with God helps you grow.

So being alone with God is a must,
For life is unsure, there's no one to trust-
Except our great God in Heaven above,
Who waits to bestow His gifts and His love!

The price may seem great, it may cost you dear,
But being alone with God draws you near
To His heart it's there you'll find He is true,
And He'll be the One to carry you through!

A Test

So many times while in distress,
It seems that God will bring a test-
To see if we will walk alone,
Or stay close by those in our zone!

For comfort causes no recluse,
Its harbor's small and scarcely used-
Not many will abandon this,
And so God's will we often miss!

It seems we're happy and content
To be a part, rather than sent-
For sending means we get outside
The box, in which so many hide!

But just remember testing brings
About the best in many things-
Perhaps it may appear a trial,
Yet then a blessing after 'while!

Alone with God is rich indeed,
It's there He fills our deepest need-
A test may prove to be a friend,
For there you'll find God 'til the end!

God Is Love

The greatest story ever told
Is one we hear from days of old.
It tells of One who loves us dear,
Of One whose presence is so near.

This One's the true and living God,
The way He made so many trod-
Because He gives to those in sin,
New life, new hope, new peace within.

He gives His love so glad and free
With this request, 'Come unto Me'-
And when we do, He's always there,
To lead, direct and show His care.

Yes, God is love and those who know
Him share this love where'er they go-
Because it's real and fills the heart
With joy that never will depart.

If you know God and He abides
Within your heart, you'll never hide
The wondrous love He's given you,
Because somehow, it shines right through!

How About Your Heart?

There's lots of debate concerning the heart,
For out of it come the issues of life-
As strange as it seems, the answer's in part
Left up to each one to choose love or strife!

Issues are common to all of mankind,
How we react to them may give a clue-
If choices are made with heart over mind
The fruit of the Spirit encompasses you!

What is the fruit of the Spirit you seek?
Well, let me just name each one in this rhyme-
The first one is love, then joy and next peace,
Patience and gentleness, then to be kind;

Faith, meekness, temperance; how many do you
Allow to reign over the issues you face?
If none can control the heart's point of view
You need to seek God, who giveth more grace!

Remember the heart, and give it each day
To God up above and ask Him to live
Through you by His fruit, and He'll make a way
To teach you to love and fervently give!

How Far?

There was a time when she was well it seemed,
No problem was too great or out of hand-
Then He impressed upon her wildest dream,
How far would she give in and yet withstand?

How far? He asked, would she just step aside
And let Him do a work to bring great joy-
The tension, helpless feeling would subside,
And in its place His promise He'd employ.

See, far was never far when He was there,
Though time now seemed so relevant at best-
There always was someone who came to share
The burden, bringing peace amid each test.

The distance between hope and great despair
Is likened to the blinking of an eye-
One minute fame and fortune, not a care,
Then suddenly she whispered, 'let me die!'

His smile again reminded, just how far
Would she allow Him to take full control?
He took her by the hand, and crossed the bar,
The distance that she needed for her soul!

If Only

'If only' we knew then what we know now,
'If only' we'd make it different somehow-
'If only' we could go way back in time,
'If only' today would be so sublime!

'If only' we could compensate the bad,
'If only' we'd now have memories glad!
'If only' we remembered God each day,
'If only' He would somehow make a way!

'If only' we could let our faith arise,
'If only' there would be no more goodbyes!
'If only', do you ever say these words?
If so, remember, they don't go unheard…

For high in Heaven our God omniscient
Knows all about our past and our present-
He knew from the start just how we would be,
He made a provision for you and for me!

The ultimate choice lies deep in our soul
To make Him supreme and Heaven our goal-
For on judgment day, we'll have no regret,
And 'if only' will never be used as a threat!

In His Time

God has a purpose for all of our lives,
A work must be done, beginning inside
The heart of each one, that we might find out
How living by faith is what life's about!

For some it takes month, and others it's years,
For faith to arise and conquer our fears-
But we can be sure it's all in God's time,
Just as this poem has rhythm and rhyme!

Just as the ocean tide goes out and in,
Just as the blood of Christ cleanses our sin-
God has appointed a time just for you,
To change your perspective, broaden your view!

Faith comes by hearing, by hearing the Word,
Through faith comes a voice that we never have heard-
Faith gives you courage to walk the unknown,
To show forth a light you never have shown!

Don't be afraid to take off your mask,
Let Him be Lord is all He will ask-
Yes, in His time, friend, I hope you will see
A life that is full, a life that is free!

Life Goes On...

The years and seasons seem to bring,
About so many changes new–
I watch how failing health, a thing,
That slowly takes its toll on you.

Yet even in the midst of this
Your faith and manner always gleam–
Although the younger days you miss,
Steadfast each day to God you cling!

Yes, life goes on, in ways unknown,
Still you are 'thankful' every day–
This attribute that's always shown
Proves God will somehow make a way!

For sure, though miles away, my mind
Continues down the road of 'past'–
With thoughts of yesterdays, so kind,
Life's here today, but gone so fast!

Now as I look life in the eye,
May pride and prejudice be gone–
Replaced by hope that bye and bye
We all will meet around God's throne!

Living on the Edge

Living on the edge, you ever been there?
It's scary at best, a challenge to dare
Get out on a limb or walk in the dark,
Just trusting in time your ship will embark
Upon calmer seas and light will break through,
To prove once again God's faithful to you!
Not just anyone will live on the edge,
It may bring distress or create a wedge-
For when you decide you aren't close enough
To God, you will find the going gets rough!

But oh! what a joy to walk the unknown!
To live on the edge where no light has shone-
To trust and believe that He will provide
All things for your life, for He is your Guide!
No height is too high, no depth is too deep,
Don't limit yourself, just know He will keep
You under His wing and show you each day,
A wondrous supply He'll send forth your way!
Go live on the edge and keep your mind clear,
Abundant success is hovering near!

Oh, What a Difference...

Oh, what a difference someone can make,
If given a chance, the chance they will take
Without fear or dread, yes faith is the key,
That opens the door so others might see!

Oh, what a difference just one life to live,
Seems but a moment and so much to give-
So much to be while counting the cost,
So much to do before someone's lost!

Oh, what a difference no frown but a smile,
Willing to be a strong arm one more mile-
Willing to share in the bad times and good,
Oh, what a difference if only you would!

Oh, what a difference your life in His hand,
He will control all you don't understand-
See, He is waiting on you to stand tall,
Take up your cross, while heeding His call!

Oh, what a difference when yes to obey
You answer, instead of just walking away-
Healing and wisdom so soon He'll impart,
Oh, what a difference, just give Him your heart!

On We Go...

There is no time for standing still,
There's much too much to do-
Just forge ahead and climb that hill,
Adventure's within view!

For on we go another mile,
Although we know not where-
Convenience isn't in this style
Of progress, so beware!

It's for the ones with made up minds,
For those who won't look back-
Who'll trek the roads that have no signs,
Yet never suffer lack!

We'll press toward the mark and prize
That God says surely waits-
And at each turn we'll find the wise
One bidding through the gates!

Yes, on we go, surrender all,
His steps will lead the way-
As in our hearts we heed His call,
There'll be a brighter day!

Sacrifice?

'Deny one's self? Such sacrifice!'
He said in jest, 'Too great a price-
For who should ask this of someone
Who has it all when day is done?'

'Not me', he said, 'I have no need,
To sacrifice, forego a deed
Of pleasure for myself or mine,
To say, Lord, not my will but thine!'

'Absurd, to think that He'd require
A man like me to walk in mire,
Renowned and polished, debonair!
No, sacrifice would not be fair!'

Yet in the midst of this rebut,
A sharp reminder, yes a cut
Deep to the heart, right to the soul,
'The price it takes to make one whole.

The One who loves the greatest still,
Denied Himself on Calvary's hill-
And if you know His life at all, you will
Be blessed to heed this call-Sacrifice!'

The Stirring

The stirring deep within my soul
Makes restless, sleepless nights-
The will for sure has no control,
As faith gives way to sight!

Wherein doth lie the answer deep,
To make this strain subside?
'I pray the Lord my soul to keep'
Seems but a childish chide!

Yet, truth be known, the great I AM,
The Ruler of us all-
Allows this time, which is no sham,
For purpose 'mid His call!

Sheer comfort is but for a while,
The stirring needs must be-
To forge us on another mile
Pursuing victory!

The stirring has a purpose grand,
Its gifts can't dormant lie-
To move the soul to rich from bland
Must be a constant cry!

The Toolbox

To hear him tell it he can do
So many, varied jobs for you-
Forthright, he speaks of all his ploys,
His labors, something he enjoys!

Convincing words spill from his lips,
Yet, there's no toolbelt on his hips-
No hammer, pliers, no not one nail,
Is found within his grasp so frail!

And so you ask, 'where might it be,
The toolbox that he needs for me-
He's not equipped to do the task
For which he does so bravely ask!'

Now see the parallel this rhyme
Has somehow quickly brought to mind-
Ambition says that we must go
To light the world, to let them know!

But not without God's Word within,
The blind can't lead the blind from sin-
To be a tool from God's toolbox,
You best prepare for life's hard knocks!

The Way

Life becomes a toil at times,
It seems the sun will never shine-
You stand alone to face the trials
That are caused by satan's wiles!

Is this the way you feel today?
Then let me point you to 'The Way'
To peace and life abundantly,
'The Way' was made on Calvary.

A man called Jesus loved you so
'Til He was willing alone to go
Through pain and torture, grief and strife,
That you might have eternal life!

When you accept Him as your Lord,
And live according to His Word-
You'll find life's toils have come to cease
And in their place an inner peace!

Trials may come, but have no fear,
The reason is to draw you near
To Him, you'll never walk alone,
A greater 'Way' you've never known.

There Is a Rest

'Where will you go from here?', he asked,
Not knowing what to say-
She smiled and answered, 'I'll just bask
In God's great arms today!
For only He knows why this time
Has come to draw me near,
He brings a rest to heart and mind,
Tho' foggy now, soon clear!
There is a rest that only He
Provides and at its best,
It's much the same and may well be,
But not without a test.
For testing is for vile and pure,
And though this seems surreal
It has a purpose, this I'm sure,
And through it I will heal!'
He slowly nodded and agreed,
As though he could relate-
For in this rest she would be freed
And ready for the wait!

There's Nothing to Lose

There's nothing to lose when all has been lost,
There's nothing to count when there is no cost-
Life has new meaning when all becomes nil,
This only happens with death to self-will!

When does one comprehend loss is for best,
Or even that living for God is a test?
Not until pride is destroyed deep within,
It is the root that produces all sin!

Pride says there's no way to give up and lose,
Give up your life is a choice that you choose-
Yet giving up that which means most to you,
Produces a yield of something brand new!

It takes one to higher ground than before,
It changes perspective, opens a door
That never would be were it not for loss,
Yes, just ask the One who took up a cross!

There's so much to gain if willing you'll be
To lose sight of self and things that you see-
Surely in losing you'll find that you win,
For God will make something of nothing again!

What Might Have Been

There may be times of sad resolve
Because of things unseen-
The best to come for all involved
Is when God intervenes!

It's easy for us all to do
The every day routine-
But then the trouble we ensue
May drive a wedge between!

Before all's said and done we find
The thing that might have been-
Brings heartaches, tears and words unkind
So different now than then!

What might have been may now not be,
Our God knows best for all-
He knows our future and can see
What makes us rise or fall!

So keep us, Lord, within your will
And help us not to grieve-
For there will be another, still,
If only we'll believe!

What's that in Your Hand?

What's that in your hand, a rod or some seed?
Perhaps it's a light for others you'll lead-
Remember the rod was used as a sign,
The seed used to sow to all of mankind.

The light of the world is Jesus we know,
Now given for us to share as we go-
Don't let your mind dwell on items of past,
What's that in your hand? Let it become vast!

For youth it may be a rock and a sling,
To conquer your foes and fulfill your dreams-
But then as you age, it may be you find
You hold in your hand, a new frame of mind!

No matter the time in life it is sure,
For hands that are clean and heart that is pure
He'll always provide, God won't let you down,
Some thing in your hand can always be found!

So take it each day and share it with those
You pass on the street, with someone God chose
To let you embrace and helping to see,
That in their hands, too, God's longing to be!

Section – VI
Inspiration & Love

LOVE   **JOY**

PEACE

Life Is a Portrait

Life is a portrait we paint day by day,
Stroking the canvas with colorful hue-
As passion and purpose are put on display,
Various poses and scenes come to view.

First we see childhood, so tiny and sweet,
Teenagers recklessly killing their peers-
Next come adults who are walking the streets,
Followed by seniors with all of their fears.

Each phase of life brings a various tint
Of colour we add to this portrait sublime-
When looking steadfastly we see with a glint,
Life marches on through this thing we call time.

Paint your life boldly and be not afraid,
Let colour abound on your canvas so bright-
When others behold what life has portrayed
Your picture will glow to them in the night!

Little Things

It's little things in life that mean so much,
Like a card or a call, even a touch
Ministers healing to someone in need,
Sharing God's love doesn't take a great deed!

It may be a song, it may be a smile
That brightens the day and makes it worthwhile-
We just never know who's waiting somewhere,
Needing to know that there's someone to care!

It's not just the poor who need to be told
That little things matter much more than gold-
For houses and riches don't fill the bill
Like 'do unto others' everyday will!

So don't be consumed by living too fast,
You might miss your moment, feeling aghast!
Questioning, 'where did that little thing go
That I was to do, to let my love show?'

Go do it today, and do it with pride,
No matter how small, you'll feel good inside-
If you'll be faithful in all that you do,
'A crown of life will be waiting for you!'

Only God Knows

Only God knows what you feel inside,
Only God knows the things that you hide-
Only God knows the fear that you face,
Only God knows your great need of grace!

The path of your life is taking a turn,
Get out of your box, let past bridges burn-
Allow faith to rise again in your heart,
For God placed it there, His will to impart!

Life is too short to have tunnel vision,
Give Him your all and fulfill your mission-
'Go ye into all the world' and plant seed,
Open your spiritual eyes and take heed!

Daily you'll meet those in need of God's care,
And only God knows if someone will share
The plan of salvation simple and true,
Only God knows if that one will be you!

Dare to be diff'rnt and show to your world
What faith can produce when it is unfurled-
You'll rise to new heights and daily be free,
Only God knows just how great you can be!

Passion

She wondered deep within her soul
If passion were a sin-
'Oh yes, of course', someone replied,
'Its clutches take you in!

It seizes your emotions well,
And causes such disdain-
You'll see your soul deep down in hell!
You can't express the pain!'

But no! This isn't what she wants
Her passion to embrace-
For passion doesn't have to flaunt
Or bring to one disgrace!

The passion she desires is such
That heart and soul and mind-
Has but one focus, and that much
Is reason for her kind!

This kind of person wants to let
Her passion be her guide-
To reach those whom she has not met
With God's arms opened wide!

Shall We Dance?

The music begins to play so soft,
And hand in hand they start to stroll-
She curtsies, he bows, as they do oft,
While in the background thunders roll.

Yes, 'Shall we dance?' seems apropos,
As trials once again prevail-
He takes her hand and off they go,
The dance brings calmness to her gale!

While dancing does she find release,
A freedom to her will and soul-
Amid the passion comes a peace
That human feelings can't extol!

Her feet take flight to higher plain,
For now the dance seems quickly o'er-
Perhaps they'll do this once again,
Not here, but on some distant shore!

So when it seems the end is near,
And life won't offer one more chance-
Don't be surprised, with voice so clear,
He asks the question, 'Shall we dance?'

Solitude

When I look into the starlit heavens,
It makes me wonder why God has given
Those twinkling objects such freedom among
The very footstool of Heaven's great throng!

Their beauty attracts the gazes of men
Through all kinds of scopes, imagining when
And how they were made, to light up the sky,
Not falling to earth, so many ask, why?

Their purpose has yet to fully be known,
But one thing remains and that is they've shown
The power of God, He does all things right,
For on the fourth day, He made them as light!

So never grow tired of watching them shine,
Their twinkle might hold a message in time-
In 'solitude' God may speak to the heart,
Revealing Himself, His will to impart!

Then just as the stars shine out in the night,
Our God will allow this life to shine bright-
Reflecting His love so others might see
That 'solitude' has a reason to be!

The Adventure

It all began one moonlit night while talking with the Lord,
The passion in my heart and mind was centered on His Word.
His presence overwhelmed me as He whispered in my ear,
'Are you ready for adventure? If so, then have no fear!'
You see, He knew deep down inside was passion on the wait
To walk with Him and trust His will, and not depend on fate!
He took me by the hand and said, 'I will instruct and guide,
No matter where you come or go, I'll be there by your side.
Don't lose hope or be dismayed when those around you jeer,
They think your life is lived in jest so soon your end is near!
But as for them there is no faith nor evidence of fruit,
Adventure found within God's realm will be a hot pursuit!'
So on we go, the Lord and I, adventure calls my heart,
And even when I may not see, He shows me where to start.
The end results will manifest all efforts we afford,
For one day soon this life will end and we will see the Lord!

The Back Burner Friend

Have you ever had a back burner friend?
This one you can find will love 'til the end-
She never takes lead, but follows behind;
Will strive with all of her heart to be kind.

Convenient she is, when others are gone,
Yet always prepared to spend time alone-
You see in her eyes the depth of her soul,
For God places there her ultimate goal.

The back burner friend has talents galore,
And all that she does for others makes more-
It's like planting seed, the eye doesn't see
What's growing beneath the soil yet to be!

She scatters her love, but focused for sure,
Knowing that loving is always the cure-
Seeking to find someone who will return
Love without measure, for which a heart yearns!

If a back burner friend happens your way,
Know that she's coming to brighten your day-
Available, yes, her love will be new,
The kind that is found from only a few!

You

A Picture of my Pastor's Wife!

There're many words that could describe
The picture you portray-
Like graceful, classy, dignified,
Yet humble in your way!

Each time you walk into a room
All eyes are drawn to you-
Your essence never displays gloom
For beauty's there to view!

The magnitude of your embrace,
Surpasses all before-
The smile that's always on your face
Displays your love much more!

Your eyes speak volumes as you look
Beyond the flesh to soul-
Your knowledge is not found in books,
Your wisdom yet untold!

Yes, you are you, you're even one,
Among a world so great-
Yet your effect is still not done,
Who knows what lies in wait?

You Can Make It!

Your life is in God's hands each day,
He's shaping it just now-
And though He may seem far away,
He spins the wheel somehow!

For like the clay the Potter holds,
Your life is fragile still-
Hard knocks in life will crack the mold,
In hopes to mar your will!

But you can make it, this I'm sure,
The Potter will repair
Your life in time and make it pure,
So cast on Him your care!

He'll take away the guilt and pain
And mend your broken heart-
That which seemed lost will be your gain,
You'll find a brand new start!

Yes, you can make it if you give
The Potter all of you-
Make Him the reason that you live,
And share His love so true!

Section – VII
Prayers

A Daily Prayer

Lord, it's a new day, You know what it holds,
I give it to You, Your will to unfold-
You know when I'm weak and too when I'm strong,
Always to You, Lord, I want to belong!

Allow me the strength to do all the tasks
Required for this day, is all I will ask-
Decisions to make, I need your strong hand
To guide me each day and help me to stand!

For only You know the purpose, intent
And reason this time in life has been sent-
So 'Thy will be done' is my simple prayer,
May I humbly bow and find sweet rest there!

Let me not conform to what others do,
But rather transform to be more like You-
Renewing my mind, so that I may prove
What Your perfect will in time may remove.

Desiring to walk this last mile of the way
With those whom I love and cherish each day-
Just let faith arise and let fear be gone,
Moving time's soon to our eternal home-Amen!

A Prayer for You

I softly called your name in prayer
And asked our God above
To intervene in your affair
And manifest His love.

I asked Him to reach down and touch
Your body with His hand
Of healing, He can do so much,
If on your faith you stand!

Although it's hard to sometimes feel
Your faith will see you through-
You must not ever doubt it's real,
Just let it come to view!

So be assured that He is near,
And knows just what you need-
He hears each prayer and sees each tear,
He's your best friend, indeed!

We love you and wish you the best
That God will send your way-
Renewed assurance through this test,
You'll see a brighter day!

A Secret Hiding Place

In younger years, I used to play
A game called hide 'n' seek-
I always tried to find a way
While counting, just to peek!

The reason being, I knew well
That those who hid were keen-
And there would be no one to tell
Me where they last were seen!

Thus, so it was when I first met
The Lover of my soul-
He taught me what it took to get
His peace and joy untold.

A secret hiding place with Him,
A must for every day-
It keeps my light from growing dim,
Each time I steal away!

I never have to wonder where
He's hiding, for you see-
When I go searching, He is there
Just where I thought He'd be!

How Long?

How long, Oh Lord, do you want me to wait?
How long will it be, how much can I take?
You said in Your Word that You will prevail
And not require more than I can entail.

By faith I can see You're guiding each day,
The path that I trod, no longer my way-
Your yoke is easy, Your burden is light,
Though weary I get, Your strength is my might!

Forgive me for sin that brings unbelief,
For when I repent, You send sweet relief-
Your love still remains when all else is gone,
Reminding again that I'm not alone!

When I look around, there's others I see
With needs greater than my own needs could be-
It makes me ashamed to even ask why,
For they seem content to daily get by!

So rather than ask, how long? Let me live
Each day with new hope and willing to give-
To rise to new heights and look for the best,
Trusting that You will take care of the rest!
Amen

Section – VIII
Special Days

A Tribute to Mother!

We cannot help but reminisce
Of 'mother dear' whom we now miss!
A tribute to her we must say,
On this another Mother's Day!

She never failed to show her love,
She trusted in her God above-
His Word was precious to her heart,
So to her children she'd impart
The fact that nothing mattered more,
Than striving for that distant shore,
Where peace and joy, eternal life
Would far surpass this world of strife!
The seeds of faith she planted deep
And prayed her children too would keep
This faith alive so all would know,
That love can bloom where faith can grow!

So, Mother, even though you're gone
To be with Jesus in that home,
You always will be special here,
For there's no one like 'mother dear'!

Christmas Time

For some it's Christmas trees and snow,
Sleigh rides and firesides, hearts aglow-
A time to be with loved ones dear,
To reminisce and spread good cheer!

Yes, all of this is well and good,
And something everybody should
Take time to do, and not neglect!
But life's enriched when we reflect
Upon the truth that God so loved,
And gave His best from up above-
A Baby born through virgin means,
A sinless life sent to redeem
The lost and fallen, doomed mankind,
See, through the Cross, new life we find-
The blood He shed was not in vain,
It cleanses hearts, removes sin's stains!

So may this Christmas time renew
Within our hearts this point of view-
The Christ of Christmas, the true reason,
He's why we celebrate the season!

Forever Yours!

Forever yours, let come what may,
This Valentine's and every day-
He knows no metes and bounds for sure,
His love is limitless and pure!

Oh, if somehow mankind could know
The depth of love this One bestows-
There'd be no tears and no heartache,
Just more and more of love to take!

His will is not to cause distress,
So yearn to feel His sweet caress-
He draws you close through bended knee,
To show how precious you can be!

Let this mind be in you that shows
He's greater than your cares and woes-
For when you think 'forever yours'
You'll find He penetrates and cures!

No need to make excuse, but find
Forever yours can be so kind-
Candy, flowers, cards won't do
What my great God desires for you!

HAPPY VALENTINE'S DAY!

For You, Mother!

Although we live so far apart,
And visits are so few-
I always keep you in my heart,
And lift up prayers for you!

Reflecting over all the years
We shared out on the farm-
At times the mem'ry brings me tears,
But God has eased all harm!

His love can conquer everything,
His blood can cleanse each stain-
And daily faith in Him can bring
A life that's full of gain!

So Mother, this just seemed the time
To thank you for your love-
The words submitted in this rhyme,
Have come from God above!

For soon the trump of God will sound,
And we'll be caught away
To Heaven, may we all be found,
On that reunion day!

Friendship

Roses are yellow, like these that I send,
A special bouquet for my special friend-
They represent feelings which come from the heart,
Feelings that hopefully never depart.

Happiness comes when you find someone who
Can share the same visions and feelings you do-
The crossing of paths has a purpose, you see,
To bring out the best that is in you and me!

Life is a gift that we get from above,
Meant to be shared through friendship and love-
So give me your hand and give me a smile,
Let's walk down this friendship road for a while!

Happy Father's Day

Fathers are special, a breed of their own,
Somehow they reflect the love they have shown
In everyday things, no matter the size,
He is 'the man' his kids idolize!

Whether it's soccer, or maybe a deer,
That's where you find the boys will be near!
Or washing the car and getting all wet,
His princess will be nearby you can bet!

God placed high value for man in this role,
Not to take lightly, but rather be bold-
Firmly withstanding all evil intent,
While raising his family with Godly consent!

This is the day set aside for this man,
You may call him father, or daddy, or gran-
No matter the name, just make sure he knows,
Each day of the year your love for him grows!

Happy Mother's Day!

Children are given as gifts from above
For Mother to nurture, cherish and love-
The love of a Mother comes from the heart,
So let come what may, it never departs!

Mother looks well to the ways of her home,
Hoping that none of her children will roam
Too far away from their Mother's strong arm,
That which protects them and keeps them from harm!

Though weary from working all day with your tasks,
You seldom say no to a deed when you're asked-
One in a million, yes Mother of mine,
Through good times and bad you let your love shine!

Arise up and call you blessed indeed,
For you are the one who cares for our need-
You love us in spite of all that we do,
And you only ask that we love you, too!

So hats off to Mother on this Mother's Day,
You truly deserve to hear loved ones say-
'Mother, you're special, we want you to know,
That now and forever, we'll love you so!'

Happy New Year!

New Year's resolutions made, oh yes, now written down,
Exaggerated expectations aired all over town-
The hype and good intentions flow, like promises to make
This new year be the best one yet no matter what it takes-
The battle of the bulge is once again the public theme,
With diets, exercise and pills, don't hesitate to dream!
For soon you'll see that you have made yourself those abs of steel,
Or better yet, can ride a bike that only has one wheel!
Yes, look around and see the things that man sets out to do,
To bring about more self esteem and candid point of view..
Completely lost within himself, his focus turns to ME,
He strives each day to be the best that only he can be.

How sad! As our great God above looks down upon the earth,
He sees the degradation that destroys His mankind's worth.
He never fails to strive to reach into the heart and soul-
Reminding man that only God can truly make one whole!
For God so loved this world He gave the very best He had,
The price for sin was paid in blood that makes a sinner glad!
Yes, Jesus' blood can cleanse the soul and fill the void within,
Where once was lost, the sinner's found, his heart is whole again!
So may this be a small reminder of your new year's goal,
Don't strive for all the bliss and wonder that this world can hold,
But rather fill your life with God and give to Him your all
For soon the trump of God will sound, be ready for the call!

It's Your Day, Mom!

Mother's Day is a special day
We celebrate each year-
To show our love in some small way
To Mom, whom we love dear!

We reminisce of days gone by
When you were strict, it seemed-
Yet now we look you in the eye
And manifest our gleam!

For, thanks to you, we've come this far
And proudly take our stand-
We've overcome that which would mar,
Now what we see is grand!

Yes, Mother, you stand tall and strong
In everything you do-
Your love and care shine all day long,
There's no one else like you!

Hats off to you this day, dear Mom,
And may you always see-
What you've instilled now makes me glad
That God chose you for me!

My Sunshine!

'You are my sunshine' goes the song
From many years gone by-
And though some days bring clouds along
You brighten up my sky!

'You make me happy', every time
I see your smiling face-
'You'll never know, dear' how sublime
Your words are, filled with grace!

My eyes reflect with each new glance
'How much I love you' still-
Perhaps one day you'll know by chance
Sunshine, I always will!

So 'please don't take' these words today
And misconstrue each line-
'My sunshine' please don't go 'away',
Each day just let love shine!

Yes, when our life is full and free,
The gray skies turn to blue-
So sunshine, now perhaps you see,
The reason I love you!

New Year, Come!

A brand new year is on the way,
Yes, even at the door-
And so this poem comes to say,
"Lord, may we seek you more!"

For sure, God has abundance still,
All at our beckon call-
Yet it depends upon our will,
Dare we surrender all?

For giving up the thing most prized
That whets our appetite-
Means seeing through the Saviour's eyes
And watch Him make it right!

He'll take our pride and any sin
That we somehow possess-
If we'll allow Him entrance in
Our heart's and mind's recess!

So New Year, come! Yes even so,
May through you God impart
New zeal, new hope, desire to go
With clean hands and pure heart!

HAPPY NEW YEAR, 2008!

Thank You!

Your acts of kindness and your love
Displayed in all you do-
Have been true blessings from above,
May they return to you!

For some it seems a major task
To go the extra mile-
They just don't want a question asked,
Nor will they give a smile!

But your example of a friend
Is evident each day-
You'll be there 'til the very end,
And help in any way!

Yes, some will question and complain
Be quick to criticize-
They have no clue of Godly gain,
They see through human eyes!

This 'thank you' is sent just to let
You know how much I care-
The best to come perhaps is yet,
As God's will we can share!

To A Special Sister!

Sister, you're special each day of the year,
You share lots of love and plenty of cheer-
Of course, there are times we may not agree,
But love is the bond between you and me!

When life becomes hard I always can find,
That, sister, you'll do your best to be kind-
You offer an ear to hear my distress,
And never will leave without a caress!

Your soft spoken words encourage and bring
A song to my heart, to which I can cling-
You know the answer will come by and by
To help me endure, if only I'll try!

I cannot begin to thank you enough
For being around, when times are so rough-
Not only my sister, you are my friend-
And always someone on whom I depend!

This is my gesture of letting you know,
That come good or bad, I do love you so-
And wish you God's best for all of your days,
You are so special in so many ways!

Epilogue

There once was a man who lived near me who invited me into his home on more than one occasion to show me something of which he was very proud.

I was totally amazed when he took me into his kitchen to show me the biggest spice collection I had ever seen! He talked about meals he could cook that would be fit for a king. He and I passed on several occasions, but he never invited me to taste any of the great recipes of which he had boasted.

We tend to be like that with racks of information which we have stored in our minds. The spice of knowledge is great, but without a dash of wisdom it's of no value to the ignorant.

Every spice of poetry in this book has been used to touch countless lives. Almost every poem has been put into a frame, used in magazines, sermons or handed to someone in need of some spice in his or her life.

The "Spicer" of Life is just waiting for the opportunity to season your life and motivate you to share with others, so that they, too, might taste and see that the Lord is good!

Josh Parham, Son

About the Author

It has always been the desire of this author to publish a book that would bring honor to God and enlighten readers from any walk of life.

Thus, the birth of The "Spicer" of Life, a book of inspirational poetry. The variety of subjects that make up the context of this book reveal the heart of this writer.

Growing up as an only adopted child of older parents on a farm in rural middle Georgia, it seemed there were many nights spent with pen in hand.

The main objective of this book is to bring more perspective to the fact that God is real! Jesus truly is the "Spicer" of Life and He desires to have fellowship with His creation. As He adds different spices to open hearts all over the world, His message will permeate the darkness and bring the light of His love, the hope of the gospel of Jesus Christ!

CPSIA information can be obtained
at www.ICGtesting.com
Printed in the USA
LVHW100052021122
732131LV00001B/22